I0755924

FINISHING LINE PRESS
www.finishinglinepress.com

RAISING THE PRICE OF THE HOUSE

a memoir

by

Karol Nielsen

Finishing Line Press
Georgetown, Kentucky

RAISING THE PRICE OF THE HOUSE

a memoir

Copyright © 2024 by Karol Nielsen
ISBN 979-8-88838-569-2 First Edition
All rights reserved under International and Pan-American Copyright Conventions. No part of this book may be reproduced in any manner whatsoever without written permission from the publisher, except in the case of brief quotations embodied in critical articles and reviews.

ACKNOWLEDGMENTS

I would like to thank Finishing Line Press editors Leah Maines and Christen Kincaid for publishing this memoir. I would like to thank the editors who published the following excerpts:

"Never Quit on a Hill" originally published as "The Inefficiency of Writing," "Never Quit on a Hill," and "Write, Pray, Swim, Bike, Run"—*The Forward*

"Buenos Aires"—*Kind Writers*

"Flip Flops on Madison"—*Big City Lit*

"Ironman"—*My Body, My Words* (Big Table Publishing, 2018)

"Raising the Price of the House"—*Common Ground Review*

"Love Your Students" originally published as "It Was Time to Go"—*The Writers Club*

I am also grateful to Sarah-Jane Stratford and Lara Tupper for writing beautiful blurbs for this memoir; my wonderful proofreader, Linda Stewart, for carefully reviewing the manuscript; my sister, Cynthia Nielsen, for shooting my author photo; and my parents, Alan and Linda Nielsen, for everything.

Publisher: Leah Huete de Maines
Editor: Christen Kincaid
Cover Art: Karol Nielsen
Author Photo: Cynthia Nielsen
Cover Design: Elizabeth Maines McCleavy

Order online: www.finishinglinepress.com
also available on amazon.com

Author inquiries and mail orders:
Finishing Line Press
PO Box 1626
Georgetown, Kentucky 40324
USA

Contents

For my mother and father

"Dwell in possibility." —Emily Dickinson

NINE-POINT-TWO MILES

I was born in Oklahoma while my father was stationed at Fort Sill as an artillery officer. He left for Vietnam six months later and served in the 101st Airborne Division—the Screaming Eagles. He was in combat by the Cambodian border, in the Central Highlands, and the along the central coast of the South China Sea. He carried rice, bouillon, Kool-Aid, popcorn in his heavy backpack and his men called him the Walking A&P. He told stories of trekking through jungle; wading through rice paddies; having his chopper shot down in Vietcong territory and all of his men surviving; losing his good friend Wilson when the North Vietnamese Army ambushed his battery; and winning the Bronze Star for Valor in Battle. My father knew that Vietnam was an unwinnable war as soon as he arrived in country. He said his mission was to keep his men alive.

When my father came home, we lived in Oklahoma where the dirt was deep red. My brother and I played in an anthill and I got bit by a scorpion. My father left the army after five years of service because he didn't like the politics. We moved to Nebraska where my father earned his Master of Business Administration at the University of Nebraska, in Lincoln—my parents' hometown. They met in high school when my mother was fourteen and they married on her nineteenth birthday. We lived in a small house where I climbed out of the window in a slip that I called my tutu and cowboy boots—and nothing else. My father found me hanging upside down from a tree branch in the front yard while neighborhood boys gathered below. My father went out in his boxer shorts and nailed the windows shut.

After my father graduated, he found a job in market research for a construction and engineering firm in Akron, Ohio. We moved to Canton, Ohio—home of the Football Hall of Fame—where my sister was born. My mother caught me running across the street to get to the ice cream truck. I didn't look both ways and ran into a car that nearly ran over my foot. My mother made me sit in "the thinking chair"—an armchair in the living room but I didn't think. I was her wild child, much harder to manage than my brother and sister.

My father was transferred to New York City when I was in the second grade. We moved to Stamford, Connecticut. We lived in a small colonial and my father took the train to the city. My father later found a job in Connecticut as an executive for a company in the photocopier industry. When my father was promoted to vice president, we moved to a bigger house with a lake out back. Before we moved at the end of middle school, my father and I started running together. The old neighborhood was mostly flat with a few gentle slopes, but the new neighborhood had long, steep hills that made me cry. I'd sit down on the curb while my father waited patiently for me to get up and finish the run.

In high school, I became best friends with Sarah. She was a Connecticut state champion swimmer and I was a diver. We studied together and usually got straight A's. She dared me to ask out a boy. I asked out Matt from lifesaving class and he took me to the prom. Senior year, I sat in English class when I heard a loudspeaker announcement. "Sarah Jalet has been in a car accident. Let's have a moment of silence for her." She was driving to morning swim practice at the YMCA when a car swerved into her lane and hit her. She smashed into the steering wheel and crushed her lungs. I went to the hospital but her mother wouldn't let me go into her room. Mrs. Jalet didn't call. I was lifeguarding at the Italian Center when I found out from my running partner, Gary, that Sarah had died. I went for a run alone through the long, hard hills in my neighborhood. When I finished the usual four-mile route that I ran with my father, I turned back and kept running and running and running. When I finished, I drove the route and checked the odometer. Nine-point-two miles.

SWIMMER

I saw him the first week at the University of Pennsylvania. He was tall with broad shoulders, wavy blonde hair, exotic blue eyes, and a hoop earring. He looked like a pirate. I went to a party at the swimmers' fraternity and saw him there. He asked me to dance. Rene was a year older and he was in a dual engineering and business program. I hadn't chosen a major yet but I loved Shakespeare class where I met one of my best friends, Erin. We both joined the crew team, but I quit before spring break. A teammate had threatened to hurt me for missing a morning practice and keeping the boat from going out on the river. It didn't matter to her that I had been sick.

Rene was Swiss American but he grew up in Singapore where his father helped develop the subway. I found a letter from his girlfriend in Singapore on his desk and she missed him fierce. I never said anything because I was afraid to lose him. I was deep in love but I wouldn't sleep with him. I was raised in the Christian Science Sunday school and we weren't supposed to drink, smoke, or have sex before marriage. He was frustrated with me but he respected my principles. That summer, he wrote me a letter telling me about his trip to Bali and Java and his experiments with drugs. In the fall, I went to his fraternity to pick up the trunk I'd stored there and he said, "No strings attached." I wondered if it was my hair. My mother had complained about the split ends on my long, brown hair and she sent me to my father's barber. I ended up with a short, feathered haircut and I felt like a nerd. Rene soon had a new girlfriend, a nursing student with long, brown hair who looked a lot like me.

SPY NOVELIST

I was a junior before I had another boyfriend. I met Mark through friends from my freshman dorm. He was an English major who grew up in Virginia. I wanted to study English, too, but my mother shot it down. She didn't want me to "lollygag around and read books." She wanted me to study something practical so I could get a job. I decided to major in international relations and economics with a minor in French. Mark took notice and asked me to apply for an internship to work with his father at a Washington, D.C. think tank. "He needs a woman," Mark said. His father had served as Assistant Secretary of State for Near Eastern Affairs and he had published a book about the Middle East peace process. Now he was a think tank scholar who needed help researching his next book. Mark didn't call me and I spent a lonely summer researching Nixon's decision-making process during the Yom Kippur War. But I met the editor of the foreign affairs journal of my college, and she asked me to contribute when I returned in the fall. I wrote about glasnost in the Soviet Union, terrorist bombings in France, and the crushing foreign debt in Brazil and Mexico. I went on to have a long career as a journalist—covering Latin America, the Middle East, New York City, and international business and finance. Years later, Mark came to New York City to celebrate the publication of our first books. Mine was a memoir about my marriage to an Israeli man and the trauma of the Gulf War. His was a spy novel set in Afghanistan during the war with the Soviet Union. We went for drinks and he pressed me: "Are you in the CIA?" "No," I said. "Come on, you can tell me. My father was in the CIA." Looking back, I wondered if that's why the CIA tried to recruit me toward the end of college. The middle-aged woman who interviewed me had vampire pale skin with unfortunate pockmarks. Mercifully, I didn't get called for a second interview. I could have ended up as a spy.

BUENOS AIRES

I met Mateo at a crew fraternity party after Erin went off to find a beer. By now, Erin was the captain of the women's crew team and she had hopes of making the Olympic team. Mateo and I danced to one song and then he pushed me against the wall and kissed me. He wanted to go back to my room. I led him there. We kissed but he wanted more. I said no. He was the first boy who didn't listen. He called the next day and wanted to see me. I told him we couldn't have sex anymore. He thought I was making it up when I told him I'd never had sex before. I could have reported him but it didn't occur to me. Instead we became friends. Mateo was from a wealthy family in Argentina that donated $1 million to the Wharton School of Business so he could get in. His uncles ran a multimillion-dollar agribusiness and were kidnapped by left wing guerrillas before the dirty war. They were released after a $60 million ransom was paid—the highest in history.

Mateo introduced me to Martin, another Argentine business student who was two years younger. We studied together at the student union and soon he became my boyfriend. He told me how his grandfather emigrated from Spain and became a sheep farmer in Argentina. His family now owned an estancia outside of Buenos Aires where they had milk cows and horses. His father was an economics professor who worked in the Ministry of Economics during the military dictatorship. A secretary in the ministry was hanged because she knew too much about the dirty war. It had ended by the time I met Martin.

He was a straight-A student who often stayed in the library until early morning. One night, he walked me home, gave me a peck on the cheek, and went back to the library. I grew frustrated and broke up with him. We remained friends and when he found out that I was staying an extra semester to finish my international relations thesis, he offered me a room in his off-campus house. It was full of Argentines and they called it the Argentine Embassy.

I became close friends with Patricia, an Argentine graduate student living in the house. Martin's father had been her economics professor and he hired her to work with him in the Ministry of Economics. They had an affair after he separated from his wife. Patricia wanted to marry him and have children, but he moved to Brazil and married another woman. After Patricia left the Ministry of Economics, she became a journalist who criticized the military junta in her articles. She moved to an apartment next to a military base because she wanted it to be obvious that the military was to blame if she ended up dead.

Patricia knew I wanted to travel and become a writer so she invited me to live with her in Buenos Aires after graduation. She had decided not to finish her dissertation so she would be leaving school at the same time. I told my mother about my plan and she said, "This will be your Vietnam."

I watched a documentary about the dirty war in Argentina when the military kidnapped, tortured, and murdered leftist activists, students, innocents. By now, the dirty war had been over for five years and Argentina had a democratically elected president. But a retired general had just attempted a coup.

I first flew to Montevideo, Uruguay to meet Patricia to vacation at the Punta del Este beach resort. We visited her friend whose soccer team had famously crashed in the Andes and they had to survive by eating the dead. He was silent and brooding and his wife asked me what I had studied. I told her international relations and economics, and she said, "A diplomat, how boring, all those parties with people you don't know." I didn't tell her that I wanted to become a writer. It felt like a distant dream.

Patricia and I soon flew to Buenos Aires where I lined up couch cushions on her living room floor to sleep. I woke up at dawn as light streamed in through the sliding glass door to her balcony overlooking the Rio de la Plata. Months later, I rented a place across the hall. It had no refrigerator so I filled the bathtub with water and kept milk in the tub. I had to walk up sixteen flights to my apartment with tea lights in the stairwell when the government cut the power. There was a drought that caused a shortage of hydroelectric power and a general strike that delayed mail from my family and friends.

We went water skiing in the delta with Mateo and Martin; we visited Mateo at his gated compound outside Buenos Aires and I played squash with him; we went to Martin's estancia in the pampas and rode horses with his sisters; and Patricia tried to help me find a job. I had interviews at Citibank but didn't get hired. Then I went to the Argentine American Chamber of Commerce to apply for jobs. The secretary sent me to the editor of the Chamber's publications, Nicolas. He had been the editor of the *Buenos Aires Herald*, an English language daily famous for its coverage of those who went missing during the dirty war. I showed Nicolas the articles I'd written in college and he sent me to the *Herald*. The editor of the *Herald* threw me out. "I'm not hiring any more foreigners," he said. I left my articles with him. That afternoon, he called. "Can you start tomorrow?"

I was assigned to the business and finance section which had just lost a writer. My colleague Andrea was brusque with me. She typed awkwardly with her mangled fingers but I never found out what had happened to her. She pulled newswires in Spanish and asked me to write stories based on the wires. I had taken basic Spanish in college and after several months in Argentina I could finally hold a conversation in Spanish. I hoped I was up to the task of working with Spanish-language newswires. I had to use my initials on stories while waiting for approval from the immigration agency. I had a letter of employment from the *Herald* but my application remained stalled for months. I wondered if I was supposed to pay a bribe.

Patricia worked as a consultant and freelance journalist. When she pitched an article to the Associated Press, she met the Buenos Aires Bureau Chief and invited him for dinner. Left-wing guerrillas had attacked a military base outside Buenos Aires and he asked me if I wanted to cover the attack as a stringer. The country was spiraling out of control with hyperinflation, power cuts, the general strike, an attempted coup, and now a guerrilla attack. I said no.

My brother visited me over the summer and we traveled to Rio de Janeiro in Brazil and the Misiones waterfalls in northern Argentina. My brother came for Christmas along with my mother, father, and sister. We went up to the waterfalls and down to Punta Valdes in Patagonia to see penguins, sea lions, and whales. When my mother first arrived, she went to my balcony and looked down at the military horse corral. She told me that was the last time she was going to worry about me.

Maria came to the *Herald* looking for a job. She had been an arts writer for an alternative weekly newspaper in San Francisco and the *St. Petersburg Times* in Florida. She worked as an English teacher but she wanted to write. We had coffee and I offered her my spare bedroom. She moved in and paid half my rent—$160 fixed in dollars. My landlord didn't want to be paid in australes because of hyperinflation. My salary at the *Herald* was worth $300 a month when I started but it was losing value fast.

Maria traveled to visit family in the province of Neuquen by the Andes and she became obsessed with *la mufa*—the Argentine blues. She wrote about it for the Associated Press. I was working on a long op-ed about the political instability in Argentina and I showed my drafts to Maria. She always said, "It needs more work."

Maria shared her well-worn copy of Simone de Beauvoir's memoir, *The Prime of Life,* and I admired her free spirit. It came as a shock when Maria said she wanted to go back to the United States to find a husband and have children. She had grown tired of the chaos in Argentina. After a year at the *Herald,* I had finally received my immigration papers. I could use my byline and I no longer had to take the ferry to Uruguay to renew my travel visa. But my monthly salary was now only worth $30. Argentina had become unmanageable for me, too. When I told Andrea I was leaving, she finally warmed to me: "Now I know who the next *New York Times* correspondent will be."

ISRAELI SOLIDER

I bought a plane ticket with unlimited stops and traveled all over Argentina—to see penguins in Ushuaia, glaciers and icebergs in Patagonia, vineyards in Mendoza, gauchos on horseback in Salta. I took a bus across the Andes to Santiago during the Pinochet military dictatorship. Then I took a train to Bolivia and saw women in bowler hats and colorful baby doll skirts scaling steep hills in La Paz. I went on to Puno, a muddy border town along Lake Titicaca, on my way to Machu Picchu in Peru.

I stood in line for a train ticket to Cusco when a man asked me, "Why do you wait in such lines?" I followed Aviv to a travel agency and we arranged for a taxi to drive us to another town to catch the train to Cusco. We met in the morning and he introduced me to his friends—Uri, Michal, and Liat. Aviv was fresh out of the Israeli army with big dreams about peace. He didn't want cold peace like Israel had with Egypt. He wanted "peace like you have on a sheep farm in New Zealand."

Aviv kissed me in a church in Cusco before we traveled to ruins on the way to Machu Picchu in lime green foothills. We went on to the Inca ruins in the evergreen Andes where Peruvians played reed flutes and llamas roamed.

We went back to La Paz so Aviv could catch his flight to San Francisco to see his brother, a psychology graduate student. I took a train back to Buenos Aires before heading back to the United States. I never expected to see Aviv again, but he called not long after I got home. He had found work in New York with an Israeli moving company and he wanted me to live with him. I said no because I knew how much I would miss him when he was gone.

I sent my long story about the instability in Argentina after the dirty war to my hometown newspaper, the *Stamford Advocate*, and the op-ed page editor published the article. My mother had suggested beginning with a cartoon published in a Buenos Aires Newspaper with two Argentines vacationing on the beach. "How close we came to losing democracy," one said. The editor called me in for an interview but she warned me that covering local news in suburban Connecticut would be boring compared to working for the *Herald*. I soon found a job in New York City writing the newsletter and publicity materials for a Latin American affairs nonprofit.

Aviv went back to Israel to study for his college entrance exams. He had spent three years in the Israeli army after high school and now he planned to attend the University of Haifa. I had my own plans about graduate school. I applied to the Columbia University School of International and Public Affairs. I was accepted and spent a semester in the school but later transferred to the Graduate School of Journalism.

Aviv soon asked me to come to Israel. I went for several weeks and we traveled all over the country. We went to the Old City in Jerusalem and took a taxi into the West Bank to see the Pool of Siloam where Jesus healed the blind man. A Palestinian boy threw a rock at our cab. Then we traveled south to Eilat and went snorkeling in the Red Sea. We crossed the Egyptian border into the Sinai but Aviv didn't want to go on to the pyramids. A terrorist had opened fire on an Israeli tour bus and Aviv thought it was too dangerous to travel there. Instead we went to Masada and the Dead Sea. After I came home, I wrote about the first intifada for the *Stamford Advocate*.

Saddam Hussein invaded Kuwait a few weeks before Aviv asked me to marry him and move to Israel. I took a leave of absence from graduate school and applied to a kibbutz ulpan program to work and study Hebrew. I was accepted to an ulpan on a kibbutz near Haifa—near Kiryat Bialik, Aviv's hometown. Aviv planned to live with his parents, Moshe and Sara, while he studied at the University of Haifa. And I would visit him on weekends.

The Gulf War broke out soon after I arrived in Israel. The air raid siren went off in the middle of the night, warning us that Iraq had sent Scud missiles to Israel. Aviv woke his parents and we all rushed to the sealed room. We had chosen Aviv's bedroom because it was the smallest and easiest to seal. Aviv had put a tarp over the window with a big brown X taped over it to protect us if an explosion shattered the window. We kept our gas mask kits under the bed. We each had a mask, decontamination powder, and atropine syringe. Saddam Hussein had chemical weapons back then. We put on our gas masks and waited for the all-clear siren to blare.

I wrote a story for the *Stanford Advocate* about the mood in Israel during the war. I called the national hotline and spoke to a therapist who said seniors like Moshe and Sara were handling the war best after living through the Holocaust and Israel's other wars. Young mothers were the most stressed. I was afraid, too. I used to cry after the air raids and Aviv would comfort me.

The Gulf War was still going on when I started to work and study Hebrew on the kibbutz. My roommate Lucie, a petite dancer from France, babysat children in the nursery while I cut refrigerator shelf lips in the plastics shop. My boss told me he liked how the Scandinavians worked. "Hard," he said. He had guessed my roots from my Danish last name. My father is Danish, Norwegian, and Swiss German and my mother is English, Scots Irish, and German.

Aviv's parents didn't approve of our plans to marry because they worried Aviv would leave Israel for good. Moshe and Sara were from the same town in Romania that had become part of the Soviet Union. Sara lost family in the Holocaust. And Moshe was sent to a gulag where he survived on bread and broth. When he was freed, he went to Paris to help World War II refugees settle in Israel. Moshe met Sara in Israel after his short marriage to a woman on a kibbutz near the Golan Heights. Aviv had two older sisters who lived in Tel Aviv and a half brother who planned to return to the kibbutz after finishing graduate school in California.

The Gulf War ended after six long weeks of air raids that sent us running to the sealed room, putting on gas masks, and waiting for the all-clear siren to wail. I found out from Jeremy, a British volunteer who was one of the few Westerners on the kibbutz. Most of the volunteers were from the Soviet Union.

As usual, I spent the weekend with Aviv and when I returned to the kibbutz, I found Lucie in bed. "What's wrong?" I said. She sat up in bed, pulled her knees to her chest, and wrapped her arms around her legs. She rocked back and forth and finally said, "Jeremy rapes me."

Lucie didn't want to tell the ulpan director because she thought she would get blamed for allowing Jeremy into our room while I was gone for the weekend to visit Aviv. So we went to the plastics shop to find trash bags and then to the cow pasture to scoop up dung. We went to Jeremy's cabin and found his rubber boots by the door. We filled them with cow dung. We took showers and washed off the dung and laughed about what we had done. But I was shaken.

I left the kibbutz and holed up in Aviv's bedroom for days. I transferred to an ulpan at Aviv's elementary school in Kiriat Bialik. Aviv told his parents that we planned to live in New York and it was a blow to Moshe's Zionist socialist dreams.

I wrote a letter to Moshe in Hebrew to explain my decision. He worried that

Aviv thought life would be easy in America. He told me he thought it would be harder than Aviv expected. When I told Sara, she asked, "Is Aviv being nice with you?" I assured her that he was even though things had strained between us. Aviv studied through the weekend and withdrew from me like a hermit crab burrowing into the sand. "I hear you crying," she said. "I used to cry when I am young. But now I am strong like a good Israeli girl." The war, the kibbutz, it all felt like a litmus test and I was failing.

My mother, father, and sister came to Israel for the wedding reception and we traveled with Aviv to the Old City in Jerusalem, the Church of the Nativity in Nazareth, the Roman ruins in Caesarea, the Crusader city in Akko, and the salty Dead Sea. Aviv and I couldn't marry in Israel unless I converted to Judaism with an orthodox rabbi. Aviv was an atheist and he was firmly opposed. We could have flown to Cypress to get married, or we could have applied for a marriage license through the Paraguayan Embassy. Aviv and I decided to wait until we got back to New York.

We married at the New York City clerk's office and had a wedding reception at my parents' house in Connecticut. Things should have been good between us: Aviv was soon admitted to the combined bachelor's and master's program in psychology at City College and I was a student at the Columbia University Graduate School of Journalism. But we were struggling. Aviv had lost so much weight he looked like a concentration camp survivor. And I had become addicted to cigarettes. We fought all the time and I wanted to leave.

Aviv suggested we see a therapist. We saw a psychologist who said she was amazed that an Israeli atheist and an American Christian Scientist had made it this far. I found the next therapist on an assignment for the journalism school newspaper. She was a social worker who helped people who practiced Santeria, a blend of African and Catholic beliefs. Aviv had been a vegetarian for years, but she encouraged him to eat red meat. I was a heavy coffee drinker, and she told me to cut back. She wondered if I was suffering from trauma as the daughter of a Vietnam veteran, but she never asked us about the Gulf War and its fallout. We fought less, but we never got back to who we were before the war and I left Aviv.

PORTRAIT ARTIST

It was my first week as managing editor of the *Bronx News*, a weekly newspaper covering the northeast Bronx, when a conservative columnist for the paper called to tell me he wanted to send his henchman after me. He thought I'd been biased against a Republican candidate in a Congressional race. Not long after that, I found federal agents in my office. My editor was charged with inflating circulation figures.

While I was at the paper, I covered the rape and murder of a college student, a gang attack on a teenager smashed in the head with a brick, a state senator using money earmarked for education as a slush fund, and ballot rigging in a school board election.

My Columbia classmate started to work as a stringer for *The New York Times* and he recommended me to the paper. I carried a beeper and the Metro Section assigned stories to me. I covered the death of a homeless man outside an emergency room after an emergency medical technician failed to take him to the hospital. I interviewed his girlfriend who was pregnant with his child. The *Times* didn't credit stringers back then.

I also covered a woman with a gun to her head who was threatening suicide in Penn Station and a teenager stabbed in a gang assault in the Bronx. I went to the hospital and the *Times* gave me a number to call his family. I called and a man and woman came to the hospital. The woman looked like an African priestess in all white with beads around her neck. "*No es mi hijo*," she said. It wasn't her son. The *Times* gave me the wrong number. The next day I bought the *Times* and looked for my story. Nothing about a boy stabbed in the Bronx. I'd called the police. I'd called the hospital. And I found out he lived. "It was a miracle," the kind nurse said. "All that blood coming out of his side." It wasn't news to the *Times.*

My last assignment for the *Times* was to cover the mood in Harlem before Christmas. I interviewed a woman who had recently divorced and was on her way to a prayer group and merchants in the shopping mall who complained that business was down since Mayor Giuliani cleared out street vendors without permits. The *Times* ran a long story about how business was booming at Macy's in Midtown without including any of my reporting. The next time the *Times* beeped me I didn't respond.

I was still working for the Bronx weekly when a colleague recommended me to his editor at *New York Newsday.* I wrote stories for the Bronx Neighborhoods Page about a gospel singer who opened a church, a cult expert with the New York Police Department, and a new homeless shelter facing "not in my backyard" protests. Then my editor left the newspaper.

While working as a reporter in New York City, I kept running into a man in my apartment building lobby. He finally said, "We have to stop meeting like this." He invited me for tea. Instead we went to an old school Irish bar. He told me that he worked as a fashion illustrator and painted figures. I told him I was a journalist and wanted to become a writer. I had already begun a memoir about my marriage to Aviv and the trauma of the Gulf War.

Sean taped an abstract oil painting on my door with a note on the back asking me to go for a row in the Central Park lake. I taped the painting to my wall and waited three weeks to call. I had started to smoke and wanted to quit before beginning a new relationship. I called a Christian Science practitioner who regularly prayed for my father who told her about his challenges as a businessman. She told me, "Dear, you need to handle the thought of temptation." I never had the desire to smoke again.

Sean said he had knocked on my door to say, "If you don't want to go out with me tell me to my face." He could see my lights on from the street and he thought I was home. I always left the lights on even when I went out and I wasn't there.

Sean went to the Art Students League to paint and he encouraged me to take writing workshops. I signed up for fiction writing workshops with a man who became a lifelong mentor. I took his class over and over until the school finally offered memoir workshops. I took the class and met the women who would form my writers' group. I showed them draft after draft of my memoir as I struggled to find my literary voice.

Sean also encouraged me to find another job. He didn't like hearing about murders and political corruption. But my boss had given me Fridays off instead of a raise and I always worked on my memoir over the long weekend. I also had a night job writing news summaries for a broadcast news monitoring service in Times Square. I met good friends at that job: Josh, who became a film critic; Melle, who studied African dance and opened an educational nonprofit; and Linda, who became a documentary filmmaker.

Sean's best friends had worked with him in the fashion industry. Dylan and Sophie were newly married and they lived in our neighborhood on the Upper West Side of Manhattan. We went to their place for dinner and Dylan and Sean joked around about being gay. That night, I asked Sean about it and he playfully said, "I'm a lesbian trapped in a man's body."

Sean's mother Helen lived on Long Island and we often went out there so Sean could do odd jobs for her. His father was an abusive alcoholic and his parents divorced when he was a teenager. Helen told me that Sean's father used to call him a sissy.

Sean cooked gourmet meals and packed me lunches, usually turkey sandwiches with homemade pesto. He was frugal and he tried to help me save money. I had credit card debt from graduate school that I needed to pay off. He convinced me to give up the car my father bought me so I could report on the Bronx. Sean let me drive his beat up old car instead. He paid the insurance for me. But his car died on the Westside Highway on my way to work and a man had to push my car with his all the way to a service station in the Bronx. The car was dead.

Sean encouraged me to take his sister's beater bike on the subway to work and then do my job as a reporter on my bike. I got a flat and missed a school board meeting. My boss paid car expense, and when he found out I no longer had a car, he said, "It's time to part ways."

Sean and I talked about marriage from the beginning but too often we fought. When we broke up, Sean unplugged his phone and flew to Las Vegas to visit his sister.

A teenager upstairs was dealing drugs and there was a shootout after a fake FedEx delivery man appeared at the door. I found a new apartment soon afterwards and moved a few blocks away. Sean came to visit me to tell me that he bought land by the bay in Sag Harbor and he planned to build a house out there. He was going to live with his mother until the house was finished.

Within weeks, Sean called to ask me to be a character witness for him. An intruder in a ski mask had nearly beaten his mother to death while Sean slept in the next room. Sean woke up and scared the man off. He shattered the sliding glass door to the backyard on his way out. The police suspected Sean who had just moved into the house. He took a lie detector and passed, but the police were not convinced.

Good Cop and Bad Cop interviewed me at my apartment. Bad Cop grilled me about Sean's character. He wondered if Sean was a deviant who could have attacked his mother. Good Cop asked about my relationship with Sean. I told him the good things we shared like painting, writing, and cooking. When I was done, Good Cop said, "She's still in love with him."

JAMAICA, NO PROBLEM

I found a new job, and though it paid more, I no longer had long weekends to write. I was hired by a magazine that covered privately financed infrastructure development projects around the world. My beat was the Americas. I had a firm grip on international economics, but I hadn't taken finance. My editor said he'd teach me all about it. "It's not hard. You'll pick it up fast. You're bright. You went to Penn." He made me feel confident, the way people do when they think I'm smart; but he seemed to have so much faith in me that he barely trained me at all. After a one-day lecture on finance, he retreated to his desk; and two weeks later, he took a leave of absence to care for his dying wife. He left me in charge, even though I barely had any training at all.

Usually, as a journalist, you can become an expert fairly quickly as long as you do thorough research, find reliable sources willing to talk, and ask good questions. But that was just the problem. The deals I had to cover weren't public, so research was nearly impossible. Bankers were loathe to talk, rarely taking or returning calls. When I finally found someone willing to talk, I struggled to ask good questions. Some were so basic that the bankers would become irritable and cut the calls short.

Investment banking was rough stuff, full of macho men and their power deals. They spoke this foreign language among themselves. And if you didn't know it, you're dumb. Dumb. Dumb. Dumb. I wasn't the only reporter who couldn't stand the beat. Some took a nip of gin; others smoked a joint, or at least a cigarette. I wasn't a smoker or a drinker, so I was left to face it head on. It was almost always an exercise in humiliation. And when it wasn't, you felt so grateful that you managed to humiliate yourself anyway.

I seemed to come up with a fleshy amount of work by press time, but my big boss in London never took to me. Ever. He always managed to make me feel like the worst reporter that ever lived. Almost every week it was the same question: Why didn't you get that story? Jeremy had it. Jeremy always had it. He covered Latin American finance for the other magazine in our publishing group and he always beat me, even in my infrastructure finance niche. He should have been a trader instead of a writer. He was all Wall Street and I was all girl. Long hair and rosy lips and a soft voice I knew I couldn't raise unless I wanted to get walked out the door for good. I wrote poems about it. Being a woman, almost the only one at so many of the conferences I had to cover. I felt like a freak, a feminine mistake.

In the first month on the job, I gained five pounds. Then another five. I kept trying to keep the weight off, but by the second year I quit trying. I was a full 20 pounds heavier. The weight wasn't so bad. I'd only gone from slim to the full side of normal. What was bad was the emptiness. In past jobs, I'd had the oomph to write on weekends and evenings, to move beyond the daily grind, to ask the big questions in life. Now there wasn't time.

My boss came back to work for two weeks and then quit. His wife had died and he couldn't deal with all that arrogance any more. I was promoted to editor and a new reporter was hired under me. Julie had studied business and worked for a wire service, covering finance. She was supposed to cover North America, but she didn't come up with many stories. So I still had to write most of the Americas section. After a year on the job, she wasn't producing much even when I'd guide her through stories. I understood the difficulties she was facing—unreturned calls, a lack of information, and general hostility, especially toward women. But I needed some backup, so that I wasn't carrying the whole section by myself anymore. Julie didn't take well to my insistence that she produce more stories. Instead, she fought dirty by telling the office manager things like: "Karol went skiing when she called in sick. She sends her resume out on the company fax. She hates her job. She wants to be a novelist."

Julie was a pretty good reporter when it came to me. She only had it wrong about one thing: I wanted to be a memoirist not a novelist. Other than that she was right on. I did call in sick to go skiing. I did send out my resume on the company fax. I did hate my job. I hated it so much that I was late every day, every single day. And I quarreled with my boss in London on a regular basis. I looked at my job as an opportunity to shed some light on corporate shenanigans. My big boss didn't see it that way. He liked to keep all the bankers happy, really, really happy. And I wasn't getting with the program.

My boss put me on probation, giving me two months to change my attitude or find another job. In four days, I found another job for better pay. The editor had read my story about a Mexican oil-services deal that hadn't been bid openly. He thought it was good. Of course, I liked him already. He was irreverent. He had a goatee. He wore silver rings, but no wedding band. He definitely did not have a sick wife. I still had to write about finance, still, but this time I was covering a public industry. I could access records and press releases and the bankers were more forthright with me. It was a much more manageable beat, and though I worked long, long hours, I found more time to write. (Eventually, I would leave that job, too, and begin to work at home—freelancing for a financial magazine based in London.)

I flew to Jamaica to relax for a week before my new job. On my way to buy shampoo the first night, I met Mojo. He walked me to the supermarket and then gently said goodbye. I ran into him a couple days later at a reggae concert on the beach. For the rest of the week, he sang to me and took me for rides on his moped and fed me fried bread fruit and fish cakes and held my hand and bumped to the beat and made me remember how much I like life. One night, Mojo's Bolle sunglasses disappeared while we curled up on a beach chair overnight. Elbows on his knees spread wide, he said, "It's only four days since somebody take up my last pair." He'd left them on the beach with his Marlboros to take a swim. Mojo canvassed the area and found a security guard to tell about the latest pair that had been stolen right off the top of his head.

We went back to the beach chair and the guard brought us sweet warm tea. We got up and walked along the shore in the morning sunshine. Mojo stopped next to the waves rolling toward our feet, threw up his arms and shouted, "Jamaica. No problem." I'd seen those words all over, on billboards, posters, t-shirts, mugs. "Jamaica, No problem." That week in Negril, laying in front of the emerald and aquamarine sea, grooving to live reggae with Mojo and his mop of dreads, brought me back. I told myself then and there that if it ever gets that bad again, I'm going to throw up my arms and shout, "Jamaica, No problem." And I have, more than once.

LOVE YOUR STUDENTS

I started teaching a few months before the September 11 terrorist attacks. I had two nonfiction writing classes as a brand new instructor with the Gotham Writers' Workshop in New York City. Back then, the school advertised its writing workshops in catalogues distributed in plastic yellow boxes on the street. I was working as freelance writer and the publisher paid me sporadically through wire transfers to my bank account. I was due thousands when I reached out to my mentor who was the former dean of the Gotham Writers' Workshop. He recommended me to the new dean who called me in for an interview. We talked about my experience as a journalist and the memoir I was writing about my marriage to an Israeli man and the trauma of the Gulf War. "So why do you want to teach?" He asked. "I need the money," I said. He laughed and hired me as a nonfiction teacher.

Even though my classes were over, I wrote to all of my students to see if they were okay after hijackers crashed into the twin towers causing them to collapse. A student said her boyfriend worked in one of the towers but he had taken the day off to surf along the Jersey Shore. It was a beautiful fall day with a periwinkle sky. I didn't tell my students that my father's flight had taken off from LaGuardia Airport just before the first plane hit. My father could see the burning tower from his window on the plane. His cell phone was off and we worried about him until he landed in Detroit. He called my mother, rented a car, and drove home to Connecticut.

Gotham Writers' Workshop hosted a September 11 memorial reading and I read a chapter from my Gulf War memoir. It was still unpublished but my boss asked me to begin teaching memoir writing. I taught beginning and advanced memoir classes. I also began to teach online nonfiction workshops. I was paid very little compared to my journalism work but the direct deposit came every two weeks.

One of my students wrote about working as a dominatrix. Another wrote about surviving breast cancer. She showed the class the heart tattoo where her nipple used to be. Another wrote about his childhood neighbor running over her drunk husband with her car—on purpose. Another wrote about traveling to Cuba as the daughter of exiles. And another wrote about falling in love with Harlem years after immigrating from Germany. I published some of their work after I became the nonfiction editor of a literary magazine.

I had difficult students, too. A Brazilian student protested my ban on emailing submissions. "This a dictatorship!" he said. He became so agitated that I was worried he might assault me. One of my students had worked as a bouncer and he later said he would have thrown the student out of the window if he attacked me. The troublemaker never showed up to class again. But I ran into him on the subway, outside a movie theater, and on my way to church. He followed me into the church and attended the service.

He wasn't the only agitator. A retired doctor left a message on my cell phone demanding that I recommend her to editors at *The New York Times*. In class, I told her I had only been a stringer for the paper and didn't have any contacts that could help her. She persisted and I was fed up. She wrote a letter to my boss saying I was harassing her. He called and told me about it. Then he said he was throwing the letter in the garbage.

My mentor had become the director of the writing program at New York University's continuing education school and he asked me to interview for a job. I was hired as an adjunct instructor to teach introductory writing and later I began to teach memoir writing. After a few semesters, I began to teach the one-day crash course in memoir writing instead of the full 10-week course.

After my mentor left New York University, I asked my new boss for a semester off. She agreed but then she never gave me another memoir class. I proposed a new class—Write to Heal—and she approved it. But the class was canceled because too few students enrolled. I never taught another class at New York University. I thought that my teaching experience would help me find a tenure track position, but most universities required an MFA or Ph.D. in creative writing while I had a master's in journalism.

A writer recommended me for the board of New York Writers Resources. I was then asked to teach writing with the affiliated program, New York Writers Workshop. I began with creative nonfiction workshops hosted at the Marlene Meyerson Jewish Community Center. I expanded into memoir writing workshops hosted at the Goddard Riverside Community Center. One student wrote stories about his bodybuilder father. Another wrote about growing up with parents in the Communist Party. And then another student told the class that her father committed suicide but she was unable to write about that. She then berated another student for his very long and detailed critique of a classmate's paper. He was so wounded he almost skipped class.

I wrote a poem about teaching, how my mother gave me advice at the beginning. "Love your students," she said. She and my father taught Sunday School for decades and they took their students to lunch every week. Many of my students became dear friends. Some earned master's degrees in writing. Some received literary honors for their essays. Some published books. In the beginning, I used to read student stories aloud to my mother and she'd often say there was no hope for the work. But I always made lots of suggestions and I'd see papers go from thin, scattered drafts to polished, publishable pieces.

RAISING THE PRICE OF THE HOUSE

He came home without groceries and looked like an enraged bull. I don't remember what I said or what he said. All I remember is him standing by the window in the living room, face flushed, veins popping in his neck, fists clenched. "Don't you dare hit me, don't you dare," I said. "I'll call the police, I swear." He squeezed his fists harder, pumped them at his sides. He reached for his Art Deco ashtray, reconsidered, and scooped up my vase. Violet glass, long and curvy and modern.

It was a birthday present from one of my friends. He glared, fiercely, cruelly, and chucked it toward me. It flew right past my cheek and shattered against the wall. Glass shards sprayed over my moss green couch, the one piece of furniture that made his place feel like home. I ran for the phone at the other end of the living room. He ran faster, grabbed the phone, and threw it at the wall. It shattered into pieces.

I had met him over the Internet and he seemed gentle, even keel. He worked in finance but voted Democratic. He cooked for me and nurtured his tropical fish. He never lost his temper, even when I lost mine. But that was before I moved in. He had a new job at a big, prestigious firm. He worried about his performance. He began drinking too much. Then he got physical with me. I knew this sort of thing happened to women, but I never expected that it would happen to me—a smart, independent New York woman. Now I know that it can happen to anyone—especially in a world where strangers meet over the Internet with no social network to screen out bad seeds.

I began Internet dating before most woman even considered looking for cyber-love. We had grown dependent on the Internet to send email, search for anyone and everything, pay bills, and buy almost anything. But the idea of finding romance online was still a little creepy and weird. It wasn't my idea. It was my mother's. She thought that I wasn't making an effort to find the right guy. So she wrote a blurb about me—attractive, New York City writer who likes running, independent films, and foreign travel. She had my sister, an art school graduate, take digital photos of me. I posed in my parents' backyard, a rolling Connecticut hillside loaded with fall foliage. I was wearing a turtleneck, down vest, and jeans. "You look like an Eddie Bauer model," one guy said. Later, I used a shot wearing a leather necklace with a large, round silver medallion.

"Your mother is pimping you out," a colleague said. She was a recent college grad who lived in Brooklyn and listened to underground bands, and she thought that only eager-beaver losers dated online. At first, she looked at me with curious pity as she watched me sift through the men my mother would send to me—usually clean-cut, all-American boys. Later on, my colleague told me she met a guy through eHarmony. They weren't sending her enough men, so she had to complain.

I wasn't looking for just anyone because I was divorced from someone I thought was going to be my life-long soulmate. I felt no rush to find another. I didn't have strong maternal instincts, either. Besides, I was already dating someone. We met while I was training for my first marathon. I kept seeing him—dark, handsome, fit—smiling at me as we ran laps around the Central Park reservoir. We met at the water fountain on my sixteenth mile.

He was my type—athletic, low-key, intelligent. He had practiced medicine in Uruguay, but became a physical therapist once he moved to New York. Talk was easy, entertaining, whether it was about marathons or Borges. He was divorced, too. He once came home with lipstick on his collar. It was only a kiss, he said, but his wife left him anyway.

My mother was determined to find me a better man on the Internet. She ran her own computer tech support business and thought the right guy must be out there if only she searched for him methodically like a dogged detective. My mother surfed free sites, like AOL and Yahoo! personals, instead of subscription services like Match. She'd cull through thousands of profiles, sometimes until the early morning hours, to find a handful of dateable men.

I fell in love with the first one. He was a marathon runner and a writer with a gentle, unaffected, flowing style. I was sure he was the one, even though I couldn't tell what he looked like from his photo. It was so fuzzy I couldn't see his face. I could only see that he was slender, had darkish hair, and was sitting on top of a desk in jeans, a sweatshirt, and sneakers. He looked unpretentious, athletic. He asked me to run the Florida Marathon on New Year's Eve. It was my kind of romance.

Then we met.

I'd suggested the Coffee Shop in Union Square. He arrived late and grimaced. It was too much of a scene, so we went to a low-key coffee house up the street. I was surprised by his pock-marked skin and receding hairline. I might have been able to get past his looks if he had been as gracious as his online prose. But he was bristly, sarcastic, and boring. I didn't give him my number. I set a rule. No falling in love until you meet them. It wasn't an easy rule to follow.

My mother sent me another match. He was also a marathon runner and a producer for sports TV. His photo was sharply-focused, like a professional headshot. He was good-looking, clean-cut. We met at a Japanese restaurant and he was easy to spot, though he seemed more compact than I'd imagined. The waitress brought us to our table. A friend from elementary school was sitting next to us. He smiled and without saying a word, got up, and left with his date.

It turned out to be a good date. He was warm and chatty, but there was no chemistry—that intangible thing that makes people want to touch each other, hang on each other's words, uncover the workings of their soul. A guy from work said he'd never date online. "I like to eyeball 'em first," he said, grinning big.

My mother was not deterred. She sent me a computer techie who liked to snowboard. We met for lunch at South Street Seaport and had pizza on the pier. He asked, "Do you have a cat or a dog?" "A cat," I said. He pointed to the swath of orange fur on my pants. He was shorter than I'd hoped, but he had spunk. He emailed right after lunch, enthusiastic about our date. I sat on it for the weekend and returned his email Monday morning. He never wrote back.

I told my mother not to send me any more men. I wanted to meet someone the old-fashioned way. I met a runner during a half marathon. He was a little young for me, but he was a Columbia graduate who was an aspiring screenwriter. He was tall, athletic, handsome, and I was into him. Then he told me he smoked pot all the time after his girlfriend dumped him. He said it was "totally bad and just a phase." Now all he did was mushrooms to bond with his friends. He seemed like a high school kid.

A friend took me to a coffee shop on the Upper West Side that had a dating service. You filled out a questionnaire about your looks, profession, hobbies, likes and dislikes, and filed it in a binder notebook. There were no photos.

The first guy who requested a date with me was a tall, good-looking born-again Christian. He seemed disappointed that he couldn't convert me. The next guy was a tall, handsome, triathlete who had a teaching gig at a university. But I was put off by his t-shirt. It was shiny and tight. I left after forty-five minutes. I had begun to see a pattern: there was always some "Seinfeld"-like flaw. I had more empathy for the men I'd met offline.

He didn't ask me out again but I kept seeing him around—running in the park, biking in the park, on the subway pouting at me. He seemed like he was hurt that I'd walked out on our first date. I thought the Universe was trying to tell me something. So I requested a date with him.

This time he wore a polo shirt. He was upbeat, and so was I. He programmed my number into his cell phone. He took me out to dinner, asked me to swim with his triathlete buddies, and invited me to a party at his apartment. Then he told me that he was going out of town for a month. He was a grad student and he had a fellowship in Massachusetts. He got my email address. The September 11 terrorist attacks came a few weeks later. I never heard from him. I decided to invite him to a reading I was doing in honor of those who had died in the twin towers attack. I was reading a chapter of my memoir about the collapse of my marriage to Aviv in the wake of the Gulf War. I called and left a message, but his voicemail said he was away doing a fellowship and would get in touch soon. He never did.

I cried over him as if we were star-crossed lovers. I wished that I could go back to the apathetic divorcee. I felt vulnerable, naked, alone. I began to want somebody—somebody right. I got back online.

The coffee shop now had an internet dating site that allowed you to exchange photos. I don't remember who I met first, but there was a black filmmaker who said he preferred white women, a former banker and aspiring poet who had a fixation with Hollywood bisexuals, and an Upper East Side conservative who seemed eager to find a wife. Then I met the guy who carried a sketch book. He was tall and thin with unusual looks. I liked him until he was rude to a bartender. He said if he'd known the beer was going to be so expensive he would have stayed at home and drank by himself.

Maybe it was a numbers game to find a tall, athletic, handsome, smart, kind man who liked to cook. I went back to the coffee shop and found another man. He looked stocky in his photo, but in person he was gaunt. He told me he lost weight after his divorce. He gave me his card and it sat on my desk for three weeks. Finally, I decided to call. He had seemed plain on the first date, but now he dressed like a J. Crew model in a suede blazer. A woman in my building winked as we left, and later said, "I totally approve." He had more flesh on him, and his cheeks were rosy. He came from old money. His father was an Ivy League man who raced cars and hunted game. His mother was a docile beauty. He called her a "pleaser." We dated for a few months, then he became uncomfortable when he found out that I'd gone to the University of Pennsylvania. "You never told me," he said, as if I'd revealed something dark and secret. He broke up with me a few days before I ran the New York City Marathon. He said I reminded him of his father. He wanted a "pleaser" like his mother.

I grew tired of the Internet and thought about the places I met men in a natural, offline way. Work, bars, nightclubs, my apartment building, the park, road races, road trips, the subway, the street. I liked meeting men this way. We usually had something in common and I could sit back, observe, get to know them a little before going on a date. I dated a colleague at my job teaching writing, but it didn't last. Then I dated a guy I met at a SoHo nightclub—an East German who was about to graduate from law school in New York. We went out to dinner. We went dancing. He was tall, good-looking, smart, funny, but he was heading back to Germany soon.

I got back online and found a guy who looked like the East German. His ad read: Chef seeks missing ingredient. He was a tall, good-looking, athletic banker who had worked as a cook during college. He said he was looking for a brilliant, beautiful, and witty woman. I emailed him late at night and he wrote back first thing in the morning. We set a date for a movie and dinner.

He looked like a cross between a surfer and the Marlboro Man. He was upbeat, talkative, funny. I wanted to kiss him in the movie theater, but I didn't think it was a good idea on the first date. He asked me out again, and again, and again, and six months later he asked me to move in. I said no because moving in was such a big step. But we spent every night together, almost always at his place—a big, loft-like one-bedroom. A few weeks later, I sublet my apartment and moved in.

He began a new job at a big, prestigious financial institution and he was under a lot of stress. He became distant and I felt confused. We had a big party on my birthday, and most of my friends were impressed by his charm and his big apartment. But one friend later told me that he reminded her of a character from the "X Files" who murdered women and kept their nails and hair. After the party, we had a refrigerator full of leftover beer. He drank it all in a few weeks. I hadn't noticed the drinking before. Now he drank every night. It made me feel isolated, lonely.

We began to fight—sometimes about important things, like his drinking and distance, and sometimes about little things, like his new habit of sticking his tongue out at me. It could have been playful, but there was something cruel about it. I kept telling him to stop. But it only got worse.

He stuck his tongue out on a cab ride home after a romantic dinner because he said he had to get to bed early. Once we got home, he lay on the bed reading my *New Yorker*. I wanted to move out, but I had nowhere to go. I felt trapped. I cried and asked him why he did it. He told me to grow up. I jumped on the bed, straddled him, and pounded on his chest. He grabbed me, dragged me into the living room, threw me down on the couch, and pinned me there. He wanted me out of there, too. I said I'd go if he let me get my wallet, cell phone, and shoes. He pushed his whole weight on top of me—a meaty 200 pounds—and pinned me by my wrists. I had to claw my way out from under him. I grabbed my purse, cell phone, some shoes and sprinted out of there.

I called home as soon as I got to the street. I told my mother we had a bad fight, that I needed to come home. I didn't tell her what happened. It was nearly midnight and the street was quiet. I heard someone behind me, turned around, and there he was. He told me to get off the phone. I told my mother what was going on. She said to stay on the line and catch a cab to the train station. I did.

The phone calls began before I arrived at the train station. I let them go to voicemail. Once I was on the train, I took his call and told him that I was on my way to my parents. He told me if I didn't come back he was going to put my stuff on the street and take my cat to the pound. I felt like somebody had just threatened my baby. I said I'd call his office if he touched my cat.

I woke up in the morning to a tender, heartfelt message from him. It softened me. I didn't tell my mother how I'd pounded on his chest, how he'd pinned me to the couch, how he wouldn't let me get my wallet and cell phone and shoes. I didn't tell her, mostly, because I blamed myself for provoking him. I couldn't believe that my gentle, teddy bear had done those things. I thought it would never happen again.

He invited my parents to dinner. He said he wanted to cook for them. That morning he bought only coffee instead of the usual croissant for me and a scone for him. I complained and it turned into a blow out. I took my journal, went to a coffee shop, bought a croissant, and wrote until I felt calm again. When I got home he looked sheepish, like he had been drinking. I told him not to drink.

We left for the grocery store and on the way he encouraged me to become friends with the neighbors, a French couple about to have their first child. I didn't want to make friends with them. It escalated and as I walked away he called me a cunt. I went back to the apartment. When he came home without groceries I knew he was going to blow.

I ran to the bathroom and locked myself inside. I thought about calling for help from the window but sat still. My cell phone was in my purse hanging from the closet door by the bathroom. I waited until it was silent. I opened the door, grabbed the bag, and locked the bathroom again. I called my parents and left a message. Then I called the police. My mother called back on her cell phone. She was already in the car with my father, sister, and brother-in-law. I had an army coming to help me move out.

When the police came, I stepped out of the bathroom, still wary. They questioned my boyfriend in the living room, and they moved me to the other end of the room to question me. "You look like you're in great shape, I bet you could kick his ass," the cop said. The police told my boyfriend to leave so that I could move out. They said to call if I had any trouble. After they left, my boyfriend tried to get in, but I had locked the deadbolt.

By the time my family arrived, my boyfriend had stopped trying to get into the apartment. We packed and moved everything, except my couch covered with shards from the broken vase and my grandmother's antique secretary, desk, and armchair. I would have to move them out while he was at work the following day. I left him a note saying: Sorry, it didn't work out, let's move on, please don't contact me.

He began calling and sending emails right away. I finally replied to an email and said, If you contact me again consider yourself a stalker. He didn't contact me after that. But he posted his profile on match.com again, only this time he said he was looking for a woman who doesn't run away from problems.

I left the city for a while to live with my parents. I commuted to teach writing workshops, trained for triathlons, and paid off my credit card debt. I still had my apartment in the city, but I'd decided to continue to sublet it even though the Canadians had gone home. I liked palling around with my mother and father. One morning, my mother woke me early and said, "Your father and I have thought this over and we think it's time for you to own your own home." She said that they planned to sell their investment condo in Connecticut, and they could help me buy a place in the city.

It took months of looking before we found the right apartment. We made an offer that day. It took a month to get an interview with the co-op board, another to gain approval, and another to close on the sale. During that time, I kept worrying that I might not get the place, or that if I got it, I'd be lonely once I moved back to the city. I had grown used to having family around. My mother told me many stories to lift my spirits, but the one that stuck was about a family friend who needed to sell her Connecticut home because she and her husband planned to move to Florida. It had been on the market for months and nobody was interested. Finally, the real estate agent said, "Look lady, you're going to have to lower the price of the house." This was a woman of great integrity and deep faith. She thought about it overnight and came back to the agent and said, "No, I'm going to raise the price of the house." It sold the next day.

FLIP FLOPS ON MADISON

It was a modestly priced one-bedroom in a charming townhouse near the Metropolitan Museum of Art and I was deeply in love, even though I could see all of its flaws. The baseboards didn't line up with the floor. The oak parquet had dry rotted and squeaked. The ceiling rippled like the top of a birthday cake. The pink-and-black bathroom was well past its prime. And the mustard laminate kitchen simply had to go. But my instincts raged: This is the one.

It looked so much like my Upper West Side rental that I immediately felt at home. It had everything I was looking for, and more. At $320,000, it was a steal. It had low maintenance and free laundry. It also had plenty of natural light, 11-foot ceilings, long windows, and a lovely view of the manicured townhouses across the street. I could see a Romanesque statue in one of the patios and a cherry tree right below my living room windows. It bloomed pink, like those on Park Avenue, a few weeks after I closed.

Now, every time I leave my Upper East Side apartment in flip flops, I think of that Rufus Wainwright song about wearing flip flops on Fifth Avenue. The first time I'd heard it, I thought, Dude, what are you doing on Fifth Avenue with all those rich, pretentious people? Who cares what you're wearing? (I had missed the part about him being drunk.) Rufus was opening for Roxy Music at Madison Square Garden and I was already impatient for Brian Ferry to begin. "Flip flops on Fifth?" I said. "You call those lyrics?" My wise and pithy friend Josh shot back: "The personal is political."

I used to think of the Upper East Side as the exclusive turf of the old boys' network and the Junior League, frat boys and sorority girls, old money snobs and new money snobs, Republicans and right-wing conservatives, and a whole lot of white people. It wasn't for me. I wanted to be around liberal-minded people who didn't care about money or its trappings, independent thinkers who never had anything to do with a fraternity or sorority, and lots of people who were different from me. I wasn't far-out enough to live downtown, so naturally, I picked the Upper West Side where I lived happily in rent-stabilized apartments for a decade.

It was the early 90s and I lived on a street that buzzed all night long—West 83rd between Columbus and Amsterdam. There were 24-hour parking garages up and down the street. There were occasional late-night police visits to my neighbors—sometimes for domestic abuse, and others for possession of crack.

My super died of an overdose in the adjoining building and nobody found him for four days. Maybe it should have bothered me, but it didn't.

I liked the place—the energy, the excitement. I liked the Cuban diner across the street where I could buy scrambled eggs and home fries for $2.50, a meal that was often my dinner. I liked the fact that the Palestinian guys at the deli knew my name and treated me like one of their daughters. I liked the way Puerto Rican boys sat on my stoop and played their boom box until the wee hours of the night. It was cool. It was alive. It was the Upper West Side. The old Upper West Side.

Then sometime during the mid-90s, when the Internet economy was booming and everyone seemed to have a good job, everything changed. Lincoln Center became a hub of superstores—Tower Records, Barnes and Noble, Victoria's Secret, Gracious Home, and the multiplex Lowe's. Apartments began to rent for double and triple what they had a few years earlier. People dressed better, even on the weekends. And nail salons began popping up all over the place.

Somehow, I found the nail salons the most disturbing. "I've got to do a story about all these nail salons," I said to Ron, a former classmate from Columbia School of Journalism. He has always been a good sounding board. Ron smirked, like a tough editor, treating all story ideas as guilty until proven innocent. "Nail salons? So, what's your angle?" "I don't know, there are just so many of them."

I couldn't pinpoint exactly what it meant at the time. But it soon became clear. The salons were only a starting point. It meant that the once artsy Upper West Side was being overtaken by yuppies with buffed nails, spiffy suits, and briefcases—corporate-looking types coming and going from apartment buildings like mine. These were people I associated with Wall Street or the Upper East Side. What were they doing in my neighborhood?

But I had to admit that I, too, had changed. I'd gotten a better job, moved into a better apartment, and had to dress up for work. At first, this was excruciating. I was used to wearing black turtlenecks, faded Levi's, and combat boots for street-reporting jobs and came to feel constricted in blouses, skirts, and slacks for my magazine desk job. Whenever I tried to sneak in a bit of soul and comfort from time to time, it never went over well.

Like the time I was reprimanded by the publisher, via email, for wearing flip flops to work. "You're the editor and you don't want to set a bad example," the publisher wrote. But these were expensive mules, not flip flops. I wanted to defend them like the champion lacrosse players who had recently worn "nice" flip flops to the White House. Still, the point wasn't lost on me. I needed to clean up my act or get better at pitching freelance work, which seemed like a long shot considering I couldn't even convince my friends that I had good ideas. So I wore heels to work, like everyone else.

I wasn't looking to buy, at first. Initially, I was drawn to the Upper East Side because of my sister's cheap apartment. Both of us had rent-stabilized apartments that went for about the same amount, but hers was a two-bedroom railroad with a big, new kitchen in the East 90s and mine was a slightly, run-down one-bedroom in the West 70s. She offered to turn the lease over to me after she and her husband bought a Tribeca-like loft in Vinegar Hill—a fast-developing Brooklyn neighborhood that's become popular among hipsters. (They have since sold that place and bought a townhouse in Crown Heights, like other pioneering hipsters.)

I didn't take my sister's apartment, but I did take a new look at the neighborhood I had trashed for so long. I went to Bloomingdale's and discovered that it was almost like shopping in SoHo, only I didn't get wet when it rained. I worked out at the Equinox in the East 60s and liked its low-key, spa vibe. And I was caught off guard by the timeless elegance of the townhouses between Fifth and Third, as I took the bus across town to teach writing workshops. The neighborhood seemed so clean and orderly and safe and, for the first time, that appealed to me. I had always thrived on chaos and dirt and danger, but that was before September 11, 2001. So when my mother called to say that she and my father were selling their investment condo in Connecticut, and that they could help me buy a place in the city, I knew exactly where I wanted to be. The Upper East Side. It's grown on me so much that I've now come to consider my new turf the best part of town.

True, the Republican Club is a few blocks away, and the Junior League is down the street, and I still see archetypical Upper East Siders—frat boys, sorority girls, ladies in pearls. But I've come to deeply appreciate the Upper East Side because it is chock full of attractive, all-American men who are not shy about staring at pretty women. The frat-boy ogle used to perturb me when I was in my bohemian twenties, but now I find it reassuring.

We have loads of other types, too. Tourists from all over the world doing the Whitney, the Guggenheim, and the Met. Diplomats coming and going from consulates and missions to the U.N. Elegant men and women speaking languages I can pinpoint—like French, Spanish, Italian, and Hebrew—and a string of others that I can't. Spiffy art dealers and designer salespeople. Of course, there are also hipsters everywhere, like the rock stars down the street. Okay, I don't have proof they're rock stars, but they gather outside the townhouse with guitar cases, Bob Dylan haircuts, hipster t-shirts, hip-hugging jeans, and purposeful bad posture. They ooze cool all the way down the street. And then there's my neighbor, who lives in the townhouse next to mine. She's got a big copper bay window that spans the width of the middle floors. People stop to stare and sometimes take photos. You might expect an Upper East Side matron in a navy blue suit to step out and hail her personal driver, but instead it's a young mother in a miniskirt and vintage floral t-shirt.

The Upper East Side is by no means SoHo, Tribeca, or Williamsburg, but it's got its own type of soul. It's overflowing with museums like the Guggenheim, the Whitney, and the Met. It's teeming with upscale restaurants and old school bars. It's even got literary flair. While my apartment underwent renovations, I worked out of the New York Society Library, which attracts a literary crowd (although I was told, more than once, that I type too loudly). I also discovered the independent bookstore on Madison Avenue. One morning, on my way to the coffee shop, I noticed a book of poems in the window by an author I'd never heard of before. I was drawn to the photo on the jacket of windswept salt marshes. A few days later, when I passed by, I noticed that the poetry collection wasn't in the window anymore, so I walked inside. "I'm looking for a poetry collection," I said. *"In The Salt Marsh."* The clerk quietly led me to the poetry section and picked it up. "I don't know the author," he said, "but I liked the cover." I smiled in agreement. I read the inside cover, a book about nature and empty spaces. It captured the exact feeling I'd had from the cover. And the author, Nancy Willard, is an award-winning poet who teaches at Vassar. Groovy. I told the clerk that it seemed to be a good one. He smiled big, just like the doormen who nod and greet me without intruding on my privacy.

I strolled up and down Madison to window shop and people watch. Sometimes I walked into the stores, though it took some getting used to. At first, I was only comfortable venturing into stores that were familiar to me from the Upper West Side. I used to spend writing breaks roaming up and down Columbus Avenue in much the same way that Madison has become home to me now. The best designers line the avenue. Valentino, Dolce & Gabbana, Carolina Herrera, Missoni. I was intimidated. Big time.

I was sure that people would spot me as a fraud. No trust fund. No designer wardrobe. No blue blood. I thought everyone could read it in my eyes—by the scared look I wore when I'd venture along the street in t-shirts, jeans, and flip flops. One day, I called home and bawled. "Madison Avenue is awful," I told my mother. "Sweetie," she said, "that's a tough street, as tough as Rodeo Drive." My mother was concerned I might turn into a Junior League wannabe after I'd moved to the Upper East Side. She was startled to see young women strolling down Park Avenue in St. John knits. "They look like old ladies," she said. "Don't ever get that way."

I know that the Upper East Side still isn't for everyone. My graphic artist friend says it's "so suburban," and my documentary filmmaker friend says it has "no character." My gay student has even said it's "like crossing the Mason Dixon line." I know where they're coming from, I suppose, but I've grown tired of things that divide us. I want to live in a world where anyone can live anywhere they like, and I'm claiming that, with my own little slice of it. So now, I stroll regularly up and down Madison in my flip flops, embracing the good without letting the other stuff get me down.

IRONMAN

I was a naturally athletic child. I used to round up the neighborhood to play baseball, football, tether ball, hide and seek, and kick the can. I skate boarded, roller skated, ice skated, skied, and biked. I took ballet, gymnastics, horseback riding, tennis, swimming, and diving lessons. I was co-captain of my high school swim team and competed in the Connecticut state diving championships. I ran track, too.

After graduate school, I did marathons and triathlons. I swam 2.4 miles, biked 112 miles, and ran 26.2 miles—a full marathon—to become an Ironman. I did the race twice—first in flat Panama City, Florida, then in hilly Lake Placid, New York. It was fall when I did my last long ride before the first one. It was drizzling and my lips turned blue from the chill. After the ride, I popped my bike into my beat-up minivan and stopped at a deli on the way to my parents' house in Connecticut. You need lots of tender loving care when you train for an Ironman. My parents pampered me and cheered at both races.

When I got out of the minivan, two good-looking guys turned away from slim blondes and stared at me in a lustful way. I had to smile. My long, dark hair had been washed by rainwater and sweat. I didn't have makeup on and my lips were a little blue. I was in a jersey, leggings, and flip flops. I was fit but I wasn't bone skinny. I was about the same weight I was in high school, when my diving coach said I could model if I lost 15 pounds. I didn't want to model. I wanted to use my mind for a living.

I wasn't training for the Ironman to look good. I was doing it because I wanted to know if I had what it took to finish. And I probably stepped out of the minivan with the quiet bravado of someone about to do an Ironman. It might sound cocky, but the thing about sports is that you're always getting knocked down, the way I was at the end of the race. I'd battled ocean waves on the swim, swelled from salt pills on the bike, and began the run thoroughly bloated. My thighs were shot and so was my back. I limped along like Quasimodo in *The Hunchback of Notre-Dame.* My mother spotted me at the halfway mark and called out, "Pick it up, pick it up!" I smiled at her as if drugged. I wanted to go faster but could only manage a slow hobble that I now call the Ironman shuffle. A pretty triathlete had told me at an Ironman training camp, "It's the most humiliating thing you'll ever do."

I ran with an engineer during the final miles of the marathon. He calculated exactly how fast we had to go in order to make the midnight cutoff. We made it with 15 minutes to spare. It didn't matter how long it took to finish that 140.6-mile race. When I was done, I carried the confidence of someone whose body, and ego, could endure a serious beating. It's the biggest beauty secret I know.

I didn't always know this. One of my best friends from college figured it out first. Erin was captain of the women's crew team at the University of Pennsylvania. I rowed for a while, too, but couldn't stand the pre-dawn workouts. Erin is a morning person so it worked out for her. One day, after practice, she said she noticed a strange thing. She was sweaty and her hair was a mess, but every guy along the Schuylkill River stared her down like a Vegas showgirl. Erin was Amazon tall with chestnut hair down to her waist, but she didn't always get stared down like that. It was her confidence that came from rowing that made her magnetic.

When I started doing triathlons, I met an East German at a dance club. He told me he was a law student. I told him I was a writer. He said he loved American soap operas and showed me his driver's license, a hint of eyeliner like a punk. He wanted me to know he wasn't boring. "There's something about you," he fished. "You seem strong." I laughed. "I am strong. I'm a triathlete." "Yes, yes, that's it," he said. "My ex-girlfriend was an Ironman."

A little boy ran beside me during my first race. "Lady, why are you doing this?" he asked. I joked that it was for the t-shirt. And after I was done I got my medal, t-shirts, a baseball cap, a fleece vest, a water bottle, and a coffee cup with the Ironman logo. My credit card company even offered me an Ironman card. Clerks at the checkout counter sometimes thought it meant the movie franchise. I didn't always correct them, and when I did sometimes they'd go blank. Who would swim, bike, and run that far all in one day? Sometimes people stare with starry admiration when I wear my Ironman hat and shirt and fleece or say I've done the race. Sometimes they glare as if they think I wasn't fast enough or look too human to have done the race. And sometimes they correct me. "Ironwoman," they say, as if it's not ladylike to say you're an Ironman. I feel diminished by these responses, but like that long and limit-testing race, they only make me stronger.

NEVER QUIT ON A HILL

The facts of my story were always clear but the meaning eluded me for years. I took creative writing courses with a gifted, generous man who asked essential questions: Who are the characters? What is the conflict? What are you saying? I finished a draft of my first memoir a few years after the Gulf War, hoping the story itself would show me the answers, but the facts alone weren't enough. I had to dig deeper, wading through memory, waiting for hard-earned clarity.

I don't know an efficient way to become a writer. I only know that through writing you become a writer. For me, that meant writing nights, weekends, vacations while working full-time as a journalist, and then mornings once I became a freelance writer, editor, and writing instructor. I accumulated drafts of the memoir, rewriting long sections by hand, as well as hand-written drafts of a novel, a play, a screenplay, tiny Moleskine notebooks full of poems, and boxes full of leather and suede journals filled with daily musings. I also read poetry, memoir, and fiction by Mary Karr, Tobias Wolff, Tim O'Brien, and others who became exquisite models of storytelling and style.

Along the way, I turned the memoir inside out several times. The first draft was mostly backstory about working as a journalist in post-dirty war Argentina and traveling solo through South America. I showed the manuscript to a mentor who had been in *The Best American Short Stories*. She said the story began when I met Aviv, an Israeli traveler dreaming about peace on the way to Machu Picchu. The central love story between Aviv and me, moving from Peru to New York to Israel during the Gulf War, was contained in a 70-page nonfiction novella at the end. It was an overwhelming, but accurate observation. So I began again, and again.

I shared the book with mentors, writers, friends, family, and almost anyone who asked, because it was easier to share the manuscript than fumble through words that always seemed to fall short. The book didn't illuminate my emotional journey, only the surface facts, open for interpretation. There were many. I was better at developing scenes and images than talking about my messy, messy feelings. A terrible struggle, for me, because I was still confused by my own story. How had I gone out for a big adventure and fallen in love only to have everything fall apart during the Gulf War and its aftermath?

A friend met a literary agent who had worked in publishing and recommended me to her. She submitted the manuscript to an editor who handled first books with film potential. We waited and waited. Word never came. She wondered if

I had any suggestions about where to send the book. I didn't. Not even a clue. She soon bagged the agenting business and went to graduate school. I saw her a few years later, and she said she often thought of a line in my memoir when she runs: Don't quit on a hill.

She wasn't the first agent to see the book. A friend from the University of Pennsylvania had become a screenwriter and novelist. "Nobody reads books anymore," he said. He told me to stop fussing over the manuscript and send it out. He suggested that I send it to a classmate who worked for a book packaging agency. I left my baby in her sister's lobby and hoped.

Within days, she left a beautiful message about how she loved the story but had never sold anything like it before. The everyman, everywoman memoir was still new, and only select agents took a risk on it. I typed up the message and saved it because her words of encouragement were precious to me. She recommended other agents–good agents, one at a time–but none of them took me on during this time when I was still trying to dig below the surface of the facts, still trying to find my voice as a writer, still waiting for my genre to find its legs. Every no meant that I had to make it better.

I dreamed of a big book advance while I was working long hours as a journalist, but I had no real urgency to publish the memoir until a steady freelance gig dried up just before the Iraq War was about to begin. I mass queried agents listed online at Publisher's Marketplace and quickly found an agent who represented nonfiction writers and novelists. She wrote two pages of advice about how to edit my memoir, mostly asking me to take out the reflection and stick to the action.

I spent months stripping away all of the reflective passages and sent back a lean, 175-page book of pure story with only a hint of what the story meant to me at the end. She didn't take me on, and that summer I fell into deep despair. But by fall, a new strategy had begun. Publishing excerpts in literary magazines.

This seemed like a winning strategy. Several chapters appeared in *Epiphany, Lumina, Permafrost,* and *North Dakota Quarterly*–literary magazines affiliated with New York University, Sarah Lawrence College, University of Alaska-Fairbanks, and University of North Dakota. Two were selected as Notable Essays in *The Best American Essays*, guest edited by Christopher Hitchens and Susan Orlean.

I didn't know about the first honor for almost two years. My mother had encouraged me to write a cover letter to series editor Robert Atwan, and she mailed the brief letter and the *Epiphany* book with a red tab on my excerpt, "Litmus Test." I adored *The Best American Essays*, but I thought it was such a long shot that I didn't look for my name in the book when it came out that fall. Two years later, I discovered the excerpt on the list of Notable Essays in a Google search.

I worked with a submissions service to find homes for my essays and poems, giving my mother unopened mail from literary magazines. I asked to see acceptances only. After several poems had been accepted, I applied to a dozen contests, including a few for full-length poetry collections. Months later, my mother opened a letter from Colorado State University. "This is a very nice letter," she said. "You should read it." My complete poetry manuscript had been selected as a finalist for the Colorado Prize for Poetry.

By now, I was ready to try for an agent again, so I hired the submissions service to send letters to agents. Within weeks, I found an agent at a boutique firm specializing in nonfiction books. He called the memoir part love story, part travel story, part war story. A challenge to sell because it didn't fit neatly into marketing categories, but he was enthusiastic. He sent the proposal to a few editors. Silence all summer.

By fall, my mother couldn't take it anymore. Neither could a talented writer who'd read part of my book and thought it was a winner. He had just sold his first book, a travel memoir, and he encouraged me to try his agent. It was a risk, because I had to break my contract with my agent. But his agent was at a big, prestigious agency, and she had sold travel, war, and women's memoirs. She read the proposal overnight and called in the morning. Passionate, excited, intense. "It's a hybrid," she said, but she liked a challenge.

For a long time, I didn't want to add historical context to the memoir, because I thought it would turn into a history book. But I kept thinking of a favorite professor at the Columbia Journalism School, who published memoir and narrative nonfiction books—one of them a finalist for the Pulitzer Prize in nonfiction. He encouraged writers to set stories in context, but I resisted until a scholarly travel writer shared his opinion that the Gulf War was a "piss in the bucket" and that Saddam Hussein never had chemical weapons.

I knew then that I had to explain the larger narrative of history and the slim slice that I'd witnessed. I already knew that moment of history intimately, but I went on a rigorous fact-finding mission, reading dozens of books and articles and documents, fleshing out context spanning World War II through the wars in Afghanistan and Iraq. It was hard reading. Memories bubbling up in uncomfortable ways. But it was necessary for the book and, ultimately, healing for me, as I wrestled with the ghosts of my past.

I thought I was done with the book by the time I found my new agent. She told me that she didn't want a little book deal. She wanted a Big Book Deal. So she made me rewrite the synopsis, over and over, hoping that I could capture the essence of my story and style in 15-20 pages. I'd send her a new draft of the synopsis every few months, wait for her comments, then revise again. She wanted more reflection. Dig, really dig.

After a year and a half of this, I asked if I was the slowest writer she'd ever worked with. She told me that she'd made an award-winning journalist work on a proposal for four years before she sold the book. Even though I had done two Ironman triathlons, somehow this seemed far more demanding of my endurance. And my mother's. My mother asked if she could try to submit the book to independent and university presses. I wrote to the agent who said she hoped I'd find a publisher for the book. My mother became my agent.

She is a techie who could have been a cyber-detective, because she can dig up about anything on the Internet. She put together a list of presses that publish memoir and mailed the proposal, using only a short synopsis similar to the one that appears on the published book instead of the opus I'd worked on for so long. Within three weeks, the editor-in-chief at the University of Nebraska Press read the proposal and asked for the whole memoir. She wrote a few weeks later to say that she enjoyed the book and wanted to send it out for peer review.

Both reviews asked for more reflection. I wrote a long response about how too much reflection could slow the pace and darken the tone. My editor suggested that I write a short letter, explaining how I could deepen the narrative. "You want to make sure it comes through to the reader," she said. So I wrote a brief note about how I could revise the book. The editorial board approved it unanimously. I was encouraged. And terrified.

By now, I knew what the story meant—the trauma of the Gulf War crushed our young marriage. But how could I force the reader to agree, after hearing so many takes on the root of our troubles? And how could I do it without making it a heart-wrenching tale? It was delicate work, inserting a line here and a paragraph there, adding a chapter toward the beginning and expanding another at the end. The revisions were a success. The press officially accepted the book for publication.

I signed books at my launch party at Idlewild Books and more after a talk at the New York University Bookstore. Then I visited the Big Blue Marble Bookstore in Philadelphia to talk about *Black Elephants* with the Women of the World Book Club. A psychologist, who spent 18 months in Iraq helping soldiers, identified with my experiences and endorsed my approach to healing. Write, Pray, Swim, Bike, Run.

My mother didn't stop. She submitted my poetry manuscript to contests listed in *Poets & Writers*. I didn't win a contest, but Finishing Line Press accepted my chapbook—and two more later on. And after I wrote another memoir about my father's tour in Vietnam and our trip back together, my mother found a publisher for the book. A friend once asked if my mother would become his agent, but she said no.

HIPPIE

I dated a pilot, a punk rock musician, and a journalism professor, and then I met a poet, playwright, and humor writer. He invited me to his readings and plays but he had a girlfriend. She was a hippie like him but they fought all the time. He said she brought a bottle of wine to his place, opened it, and started drinking alone in the living room while he worked in another room. He told me he broke up with her and I wondered what I would do to offend him. We ushered at plays and went to operas at the Met. And when I moved to upstate New York for a year he visited me in his converted school bus. And he still visited me when I moved back to my Upper East Side apartment after a long isolating winter upstate. He didn't want to marry me or live with me but he desperately wanted to have a baby with me. I didn't want children, but he persisted anyway. Then he bought land in New Orleans and moved there to build a house. When he visited me in New York, he said, "You kept me here for many years." It didn't last.

LUNCH HOUR

I found a job in Midtown writing evaluations for specialty occupation visa applicants in the name of professors of computer science, engineering, chemistry, biology, finance, accounting, marketing, fashion design, graphic design, food science, law. I am a ghost writer, using templates created by other writers, shaping and adapting them to the particulars of the case. The paycheck comes direct deposit every two weeks and, for the first time, I have saved thousands. I never saved during my long years as a journalist, working under the constant pressure to keep sources from complaining about my work despite its accuracy. After I left journalism to become a writing teacher and editor, I never earned enough. I rarely traveled, too poor most of the time, but I wrote and wrote. Now I struggle to say something poetic on my lunch hour. It goes too fast.

OPEN MIC POET

I go to an open mic poetry reading once a month and see friends like Anton, a surrealist poet and translator who hosts the reading; Robert, a poet who plays percussion in a free rock band; Rick, poet, painter, and journalist who used to work with me; and Judy, a poet and proofreader who still works with me. I read lighthearted poems about running into a bear on a hike in upstate New York; touching a giant clam that snapped shut while scuba diving in Australia; getting hit on by homeless men calling me "Charlie's Angels" and asking me to watch TV and hold hands; working remotely from my parents' house in Connecticut and streaming cop shows during the long hours of quarantine; and seeing a woman sitting on the sidewalk eating pancakes along Madison Avenue after I moved back to the city. I am always writing something new to share with my poetry friends. We go to each other's book parties. We read each other's books. We celebrate each other's poems.

Karol Nielsen is the author of the memoirs *Walking A&P* (Mascot Books, 2018) and *Black Elephants* (Bison Books, 2011)—shortlisted for the 2012 William Saroyan International Prize for Writing in nonfiction. Excerpts were honored as notable essays in *The Best American Essays 2010* and *2005*. Her poetry chapbooks include *Small Life* (2022), *Vietnam Made Me Who I Am* (2020), and *This Woman I Thought I'd Be* (2012)—all from Finishing Line Press. Her full-length poetry collection was longlisted for the 2021 Terry J. Cox Poetry Award in and was selected as a finalist for the 2007 Colorado Prize for Poetry. One of her poems was a finalist for the 2021 Ruth Stone Poetry Prize. Her work has appeared in the anthology *The Moment: Wild, Poignant, Life-changing Stories from 125 Artists and Writers Famous & Obscure* (Harper Perennial, 2012) and many publications, including *Epiphany, Guernica, Lumina, North Dakota Quarterly, Permafrost,* and *RiverSedge.* As a journalist, she covered Latin America, the Middle East, New York City, and other beats—contributing to the *Stamford Advocate* as an op-ed writer, *New York Newsday* as a freelance writer, the *New York Times* as a stringer, and others.

www.ingramcontent.com/pod-product-compliance
Lightning Source LLC
LaVergne TN
LVHW090537110826
845146LV00003B/1149

* 9 7 9 8 8 8 8 3 8 5 6 9 2 *